Spiritual Warfare Prayers For Men

Modern Edition

30 Days Spiritual Warfare Prayer Book for Men.

Overcome Overthinking, Loneliness, Anger, Spiritual Attacks and Protection from Spiritual Darkness with God's Word.

Prayer Rocks

COPYRIGHT © 2025 | PRAYER ROCKS

PAPERBACK ISBN: 978-1-965849-50-7

EBOOK ISBN: 978-1-965849-49-1

Table of Contents

INTRODUCTION
UNDERSTANDING SPIRITUAL WARFARE

As a man, you are born into a war that has raged since the beginning of time—a battle between the kingdom of God and the forces of darkness. This war is not fought with guns and swords but with spiritual weapons, for it is not against flesh and blood that we struggle *(Ephesians 6:12)*.

The enemy is not a figment of imagination. He is real, strategic, and relentless. His goal? To steal your identity, crush your purpose, break your relationships, entangle you in addiction, and keep you powerless. But the good news is this—God has already won the war through Jesus Christ. Your role is to stand in that victory, wielding the weapons of spiritual warfare that He has provided.

This book is your training ground. It will equip you with prayers, scriptures, and strategies to fight and win in every area of your life.

WHY SPIRITUAL WARFARE IS CRUCIAL FOR MEN

Men, whether fathers, husbands, sons, or leaders, are primary targets for spiritual attacks. Satan understands the principle laid out in Matthew 26:31: "Strike the shepherd, and the sheep will scatter." As men, God designed us to be spiritual shepherds, leaders, protectors, and providers in our homes, communities, and workplaces. If the enemy can weaken, distract, or deceive us, our families suffer, our churches become vulnerable, and communities deteriorate.

Dr. Tony Evans rightly says, *"You do not pray as a beggar, but as a warrior for the King of kings"*. You must understand the magnitude of your identity as men in Christ. The devil wants you passive, spiritually disarmed, distracted by the world's pleasures, overwhelmed by financial strain, trapped by addiction, and imprisoned by guilt. But you are called by God to live a victorious life— a life marked by freedom, authority, courage, and clarity of purpose.

THE BATTLES WE FACE AS MEN

Every man faces unique spiritual battles. Perhaps you struggle with your sense of identity, secretly battling self-doubt, feeling inadequate, or haunted by past mistakes. Maybe the war for you is emotional—overcoming anxiety, depression, anger, fear, shame, and even self-destructive thoughts. You may face relational battles— challenges in marriage, temptations of lust and pornography, difficulty raising your children in godliness, or the deep wounds of betrayal and abandonment.

Other battles are tangible yet deeply spiritual—struggles with career stagnation, financial bondage, workplace challenges, and even physical health issues. Addictions may hold you captive, and destructive habits like pornography and masturbation quietly erode your spiritual vitality.

Jennifer LeClaire makes a powerful point: *"Ignoring the devil won't make the warfare stop. Indeed, one of the enemy's greatest deceptions is convincing you to lay your weapons down."* Your struggles are real, and they are part of a spiritual war designed to keep you bound, defeated, and powerless.

THE POWER OF PRAYER & HOW THIS BOOK WILL HELP

God never intended for you to fight this battle alone or in your own strength. Jesus has already won the victory through the cross, defeating every power of darkness (Colossians 2:15). Yet, victory requires you to actively stand your ground, equipped and ready for spiritual warfare. You have been given divine weapons—truth, faith, prayer, and the powerful word of God—to demolish every stronghold in your life (2 Corinthians 10:4).

Prayer is the heartbeat of spiritual warfare. Leighann McCoy asserts profoundly: *"Your best defense against the lies of the devil is the Word of God."* When you align yourself with God's promises and power through prayer, you expose and thwart the schemes of the enemy.

This book is your spiritual war manual. Each day you will encounter:

- **Scripture** to anchor you in God's eternal truth.
- **Devotional reflections** to provide practical wisdom and insight.
- **Powerful warfare prayers** to declare victory over your life.

- **Action steps** to implement truths learned and to experience tangible breakthroughs.

This structured 30-day approach ensures you don't just read about victory—you experience it.

HOW TO USE THIS BOOK EFFECTIVELY

This book isn't merely to be read—it's designed to transform your life through active engagement. Daily, you will:

1. **Read & Meditate on Scripture**: Anchor your thoughts and emotions in biblical truth.
2. **Reflect Devotionally**: Let the practical teachings challenge and shift your perspectives.
3. **Engage in Warfare Prayer**: Use the provided prayers as a guide, praying fervently and personally against the strongholds in your life.
4. **Take Practical Action**: Each day's action step will equip you to integrate these spiritual insights into your daily routine.

As you journey through these pages, record your experiences, insights, victories, and struggles. Remember, spiritual warfare is real, but so is your victory in Christ.

This is your battle cry moment. It's time to rise from passive Christianity to active spiritual warfare, from defeat to victory. Equip yourself, stand firm, and experience the freedom, restoration, and strength that

Christ has purchased for you. Let today mark the beginning of your victory!

"Yet in all these things we are more than conquerors through Him who loved us." (Romans 8:37)

You were made for this moment. It's time to fight— and it's time to win!

PART 1: IDENTITY, PURPOSE & BREAKING STRONGHOLDS

Day 1: Rediscovering Your Identity in Christ

2 Corinthians 5:17 (NKJV)

"Therefore, if anyone is in Christ, he is a new creation; old things have passed away; behold, all things have become new."

Reflection:
As men, our true identity is often under relentless spiritual attack. The enemy attempts to trap us in past mistakes, failures, shame, or societal expectations. Yet, God's Word clearly tells us that we are not defined by what we've done, but by what Christ has done for us. In Christ, the past loses its grip, and we become brand-new creations—free, forgiven, empowered, and destined for greatness.

Brother, your true identity is deeply rooted in Christ. Today, break every false label that has kept you bound, and confidently embrace who God declares you are—a mighty man of valor, purpose, and strength.

Prayer:

Heavenly Father, today, I, _____, boldly step into my new identity in Christ. I surrender every false belief, every lie of the enemy, and every past mistake that has held me captive. By the power in Your Word, I declare that I am no longer defined by my past, but by Your grace alone. I embrace my new nature, cleansed by Your blood, empowered by Your Spirit, and affirmed by Your everlasting love. I renounce every spiritual stronghold that seeks to diminish who You've called me to be. Today, I rise in my true identity, whole, confident, victorious, and free. In Jesus' mighty name, Amen.

Action Step:

Write down three false labels or negative identities you've believed about yourself in the past. Cross each one out boldly and replace them with three biblical affirmations that declare who you truly are in Christ. Meditate on these affirmations throughout the day.

Daily Declarations & Affirmations:

- **I declare:** I am a new creation in Christ Jesus. My past has no power over my present or my future.
- **I affirm:** I am loved, forgiven, redeemed, and set apart by God.
- **I decree:** My identity is secure in Christ alone; I am accepted, valued, and chosen by God.

Day 2: Finding Your Life's Purpose & Calling

Jeremiah 29:11 (NKJV)

"For I know the thoughts that I think toward you, says the Lord, thoughts of peace and not of evil, to give you a future and a hope."

Reflection:
God has placed within each man a specific purpose and a unique calling. Life without purpose leads to frustration, emptiness, and confusion. But God has already declared His good intentions and hopeful plans for your life. Your purpose is not hidden from God—it is carefully designed and ordained by Him. Today, align your heart to discover and fulfill your divine calling.

Prayer:
Father, today I, _____, submit my life completely to Your sovereign plan. Remove every distraction and confusion blocking my vision. Clearly reveal Your divine purpose and calling over my life. Equip and empower me to boldly walk in the destiny You've ordained. May Your desires become my desires, and may my steps be ordered by You from this day forward. In Jesus' name, Amen.

Action Step:
Spend 10-15 minutes in quiet meditation today, listening for God's guidance. Journal the thoughts or impressions the Holy Spirit reveals regarding your purpose and calling.

Daily Declarations & Affirmations:

- **I declare:** God has good plans for my life—plans filled with hope, peace, and prosperity.
- **I affirm:** My life's purpose and calling come from God, and He will clearly reveal it to me.
- **I decree:** I will fulfill every divine purpose God has ordained for my life; nothing shall stop me.

Day 3: Healing from Father Wounds & Parental Rejection

Psalm 68:5-6 (NIV)

A father to the fatherless, a defender of widows, is God in his holy dwelling. God sets the lonely in families, He leads out the prisoners with singing; but the rebellious live in a sun-scorched land.

Reflection:

Many men carry hidden wounds, hurts, and pains resulting from broken relationships or rejection from earthly fathers or parents. These wounds often distort our understanding of God as our loving Father. Today, I choose healing. God desires to bind up these deep wounds and replace pain with His unfailing love. His promise is clear: He will become the Father I always longed for, faithfully walking beside me in every season.

Prayer:

Heavenly Father, Today, I, _____, surrender every deep-seated pain and wound from fatherly rejection and parental disappointment. Lord, heal my heart from bitterness, anger, and resentment. Be my perfect Father, filling the emptiness left by others. Settle me in Your divine family, giving me comfort, acceptance, and security. I receive Your unconditional love today, Lord, and choose forgiveness and freedom over pain and bondage.
In Jesus' Name, Amen.

Action Step:

- Write a letter to your earthly father (or parent)—even if you never send it—expressing forgiveness and release. Allow God's peace to flow through this act of healing.

Daily Declarations & Affirmations:

- God is my perfect Father; I am completely loved and accepted by Him.
- I forgive those who have hurt me; I choose healing over bitterness.
- I am not defined by rejection; I am adopted into God's eternal family.

Day 4: Breaking Free from Midlife Crisis & Lost Identity

Isaiah 43:19 (NIV)

See, I am doing a new thing! Now it springs up; do you not perceive it? I am making a way in the wilderness and streams in the wasteland.

Reflection:

There are seasons when my identity, purpose, and sense of accomplishment feel uncertain. Midlife often brings questions and doubts, but God's promise remains firm. He is doing something new, making a way in seemingly barren places. Today, I embrace a fresh vision, receiving clarity and direction, as God guides me through this transitional season.

Prayer:

Lord God, Today, I, _____, place before You all fears, confusion, and anxieties surrounding my identity, age, accomplishments, and future. Lord, do a new thing in me! Give me fresh vision, renewed confidence, and divine clarity. Let streams of hope flow through my wasteland experiences. Guide me powerfully into my next chapter, filled with Your peace, purpose, and joy.

In Jesus' Name, Amen.

Action Step:

- Write down three areas you desire to see renewed and restored. Commit these specifically to prayer daily.

Daily Declarations & Affirmations:

- My future is secure in Christ; my best days are yet ahead.
- God is leading me into new opportunities; I embrace change without fear.
- I am never stuck or forgotten; God is actively guiding me into His good plans.

Day 5: Overcoming Self-Doubt & Low Confidence

Philippians 4:13 (NIV)

I can do all this through him who gives me strength.

Reflection:

Self-doubt and low confidence rob me of fully living the victorious life God intends. Christ Himself strengthens me, empowering me to overcome fears and insecurities. Today, I boldly renounce negative thoughts and affirm the strength God has placed within me.

Prayer:

Lord Jesus, I, _____, surrender every area of insecurity, self-doubt, and fear into Your hands. Today, I fully embrace Your strength as my own. Let Your power overcome my weaknesses. Let faith rise above fear in every area of my life. I declare boldness, courage, and confidence through Your unfailing strength. In Jesus' Name, Amen.

Action Step:

- Identify at least one practical area where you can step outside your comfort zone today, intentionally confronting insecurities.

Daily Declarations & Affirmations:

- I can achieve all God has called me to, through Christ who strengthens me.
- Fear and insecurity no longer control me; I walk confidently in Christ.

- My identity is rooted in Christ's strength, not in human opinions.

Day 6: Prayers for Career Growth & Leadership Strength

Deuteronomy 8:18 (NIV)

But remember the LORD your God, for it is he who gives you the ability to produce wealth, and so confirms his covenant, which he swore to your ancestors, as it is today.

Reflection:

God desires that I flourish professionally, not for selfish ambition, but for His kingdom purpose. He promises to give me the ability to succeed, lead, and bless others. Today, I surrender my career to His purpose and direction.

Prayer:

Father God, Today, I, _____, lay my career, my leadership, and all professional aspirations before Your throne. Guide my steps, give me divine wisdom, creative ideas, and exceptional favor. Let my work glorify You and positively impact others. Strengthen my leadership; grant me integrity, compassion, and courage. Prosper my hands as a testimony of Your faithfulness. In Jesus' Name, Amen.

Action Step:

- Dedicate your workday specifically to God today, intentionally honoring Him in your interactions and decisions.

Daily Declarations & Affirmations:

- God blesses and prospers the work of my hands.
- I am gifted, capable, and positioned to excel professionally for God's glory.

- My leadership influences others positively and advances God's kingdom.

Day 7: Breaking the Chains of Stagnation & Lack of Progress

Psalm 1:3 (NIV)

That person is like a tree planted by streams of water, which yields its fruit in season and whose leaf does not wither—whatever they do prospers.

Reflection:

God's will is never stagnation, delay, or frustration. He promises fruitfulness and continual growth in every area of my life. Today, I break every spiritual chain holding me back and step boldly into a season of breakthrough and prosperity.

Prayer:

Lord, Today, I, _____, break free from every spirit of stagnation, delay, limitation, and lack of progress. I declare fruitfulness, forward movement, and prosperity in my life. I receive supernatural breakthroughs, open doors, and divine acceleration. Let Your streams flow through every dry place in my life. In Jesus' Name, Amen.

Action Step:

- Clearly define one area of your life where progress has stalled. Commit it daily to prayer and intentional action.

Daily Declarations & Affirmations:

- I am fruitful and prospering in Christ.
- Every chain of stagnation is broken; I walk in supernatural advancement.
- God positions me beside streams of provision; whatever I touch prospers.

PART 2: EMOTIONAL & MENTAL WARFARE

Day 8: Overcoming Anxiety & Depression

Philippians 4:6-7 (KJV)

"Be careful for nothing; but in every thing by prayer and supplication with thanksgiving let your requests be made known unto God. And the peace of God, which passeth all understanding, shall keep your hearts and minds through Christ Jesus."

Reflection:

I remind myself today that anxiety and depression are not part of God's design for my life. By turning my worries into prayers and offering thanks to God, I open my heart to His supernatural peace that defies every storm. I can rest in the certainty that He cares deeply for me, and that He is strong enough to carry all my concerns.

Prayer:

Heavenly Father, I stand in awe of Your goodness and love. Today, I lay every anxious thought and heavy feeling before You. Fill my heart with hope and remind me that my identity is found in Jesus Christ, not in my struggles. Help me to trust You more, even when I can't see the answers. I, _____, declare that You are my refuge, my strong tower, and my steadfast source of joy. In Jesus' name, amen.

Action Step

- List your biggest worries on a piece of paper. Pray over each one, then tear up the list and throw it away as a symbolic act of releasing them to God.

Daily Declarations & Affirmations
- I declare that God's peace rules my heart and mind.
- I affirm that through Christ, I am not defined by anxiety or depression.
- I boldly speak that the joy of the Lord is my strength.

Day 9: Healing from Loneliness & Isolation

Isaiah 41:10 (KJV)

"Fear thou not; for I am with thee: be not dismayed; for I am thy God: I will strengthen thee; yea, I will help thee; yea, I will uphold thee with the right hand of my righteousness."

Reflection:

The feeling of being alone can strike deeply. Yet God promises He is with me—always. His presence is the antidote to isolation. Even when I walk through silent seasons, He is my God, offering strength that sustains me. By faith, I choose to believe I am never truly alone.

Prayer:

Lord, thank You for being my constant companion. When loneliness surrounds me, remind me of Your nearness. Lift me out of every dark corner and draw my heart close to Yours. I, _____, receive Your strength and help now. I believe that as I abide in You, I find both comfort and belonging. In Jesus' name, amen.

Action Step:

- Reach out to someone you've lost contact with. Send a message or make a call. Reestablishing connection can be a powerful step in overcoming isolation.

Daily Declarations & Affirmations

- I declare I am never alone, for God is always with me.
- I affirm that I belong to a family of believers through Christ.

- I embrace friendship and unity, and I reject every lie of isolation.

Day 10: Breaking the Chains of Shame & Guilt

Romans 8:1 (KJV)

"There is therefore now no condemnation to them which are in Christ Jesus, who walk not after the flesh, but after the Spirit."

Reflection:

Shame and guilt weigh heavily, but I have been made free by the blood of Jesus. His righteousness covers my past, present, and future. Through Christ, my failures do not define me—His redemption does. I can live boldly, free from self-condemnation.

Prayer:

Father, I praise You for removing my shame at the cross. By the power of Jesus' sacrifice, I am forgiven. I lay every past mistake at Your feet. I, _____, embrace the gift of new life and reject every ounce of condemnation. When the enemy tries to remind me of my sins, help me remember Your grace. In Jesus' name, amen.

Action Step:

Write down one past regret that still haunts you. Pray over it, thank God for His forgiveness, and destroy that note as a sign of letting go.

Daily Declarations & Affirmations:

- I declare that I am covered by Christ's righteousness.
- I affirm that God's mercy triumphs over judgment in my life.
- I stand forgiven and cleansed by the blood of Jesus.

Day 11: Deliverance from Fear & Uncertainty

2 Timothy 1:7 (KJV)

"For God hath not given us the spirit of fear; but of power, and of love, and of a sound mind."

Reflection:

Fear is often rooted in uncertainty, but I have a Spirit of power through Christ. Even when I face the unknown, I can stand assured that my God is for me. Rather than letting fear dictate my steps, I trust the One who holds my future securely.

Prayer:

Mighty God, thank You for giving me power, love, and a sound mind. I refuse to accept fear and anxiety as my portion. Instead, I set my gaze on Your might. I, _____, speak life to every situation that seems impossible. Teach me to stand on Your Word and to walk confidently, knowing You've already prepared the way. In Jesus' name, amen.

Action Step:

1. Do one thing today you've been avoiding out of fear—whether it's making a crucial phone call or starting a long-delayed project. Commit it to God first, then act boldly.

Daily Declarations & Affirmations:

- I declare that fear has no hold on my heart.
- I affirm that the Spirit of God within me brings courage.
- I embrace a confident mind-set, knowing God leads me forward.

Day 12: Prayers for Peace in the Mind (overthinking)

Isaiah 26:3 (KJV)

"Thou wilt keep him in perfect peace, whose mind is stayed on thee: because he trusteth in thee."

Reflection:

God desires to keep me in perfect peace—a peace that saturates my thoughts, desires, and emotions. By setting my mind on Him, I step into the calm assurance of His sovereignty. Trusting in Him dismantles every worry that tries to invade my mind.

Prayer:

Heavenly Father, I fix my thoughts on You today. Thank You for promising perfect peace to those who trust in You. May every restless thought bow to the power of Your presence. I, _____, open my mind to Your Word and close every door to confusion, overthinking and chaos. I receive Your peace that passes understanding. In Jesus' name, amen.

Action Step:

- Choose a verse on peace (like Isaiah 26:3) and post it in a visible place—your desk, mirror, or phone wallpaper. Let it constantly remind you to refocus on the Lord.

Daily Declarations & Affirmations:

- I declare my mind is filled with thoughts of God's faithfulness.
- I affirm that God's peace rules over all turmoil in my life.
- I proclaim that confusion has no place where Christ reigns.

Day 13: Overcoming Anger, Rage & Frustration

James 1:19-20 (KJV)

"Wherefore, my beloved brethren, let every man be swift to hear, slow to speak, slow to wrath: For the wrath of man worketh not the righteousness of God."

Reflection:

Unchecked anger can ravage relationships and poison my heart. But God's Word calls me to patience and self-control. The more I yield my emotions to Christ, the more my anger is replaced with compassion and understanding, reflecting the righteousness of God in every conflict.

Prayer:

Lord, I confess that anger sometimes flares in me. Teach me to be swift to listen and slow to speak. Guard my words so they bring life rather than destruction. I, _____, invite the Holy Spirit to purify my emotions. Let my responses reveal Your grace. In Jesus' name, amen.

Action Step:

- Pause before responding: When tension arises, take a brief moment to pray silently, asking the Holy Spirit to guide your words and tone.

Daily Declarations & Affirmations:

- I declare I am patient and slow to anger.
- I affirm that my words will be seasoned with grace.
- I proclaim that God's righteousness is my standard for every conflict.

Day 14: Breaking the Spirit of Procrastination & Laziness

Proverbs 6:6-8 (KJV)

"Go to the ant, thou sluggard; consider her ways, and be wise: Which having no guide, overseer, or ruler, provideth her meat in the summer, and gathereth her food in the harvest."

Reflection:

God's Word urges me to learn diligence and initiative from the humble ant. Even when no one is watching, I am called to steward my time, gifts, and opportunities. By resisting laziness, I align with God's purpose and maximize every moment He's entrusted to me.

Prayer:

Father, thank You for reminding me that diligence is a mark of Your character. I repent of any laziness that keeps me from fulfilling my calling. I, _____, choose today to rise up and work faithfully, trusting You to bless my efforts. Empower me to press on, even when the tasks seem mundane. In Jesus' name, amen.

Action Step:

- Set a timer for 15 minutes and start the task you've been delaying most. Commit to seeing it through step by step until it's completed.

Daily Declarations & Affirmations:

- I declare I am a faithful and diligent servant of Christ.
- I affirm that God's strength is made perfect in my moments of weakness.
- I speak life over my plans and projects, believing God will help me complete them.

PART 3: RELATIONSHIPS, PURITY & BREAKING SEXUAL STRONGHOLDS
Day 15: Restoration in Marriage & Overcoming Marital Struggles

Ephesians 5:25 (KJV)
"Husbands, love your wives, even as Christ also loved the church, and gave himself for it."
Reflection:

Christ's love for the church sets the standard for my love toward my wife. True restoration flows when I model this sacrificial commitment—offering forgiveness, patience, and empathy. God desires unity and harmony in my marriage, and He will strengthen my resolve to love well.
Prayer:

Lord, thank You for teaching me the depth of true love through Christ. Help me to die to selfishness and pride, so my marriage reflects Your redemptive grace. I, _____, surrender every marital struggle to You. Empower me to love my wife relentlessly and to pursue peace daily. In Jesus' name, amen.
Action Step:
- Schedule uninterrupted time to connect with your wife— share hearts, pray together, and reaffirm your commitment to each other.

Daily Declarations & Affirmations:
- I declare my marriage is founded on Christ's sacrificial love.
- I affirm I am patient, kind, and selfless toward my spouse.
- I proclaim restoration and oneness over my marriage in Jesus' name.

Day 16: Breaking Free from Relationship Trauma & Betrayal

Psalm 147:3 (KJV)

"He healeth the broken in heart, and bindeth up their wounds."

Reflection:

When betrayal cuts deep, God's love can reach even deeper. He is the healer of broken hearts, binding every wound with His compassionate hands. His power is greater than my past hurts, and in Him I can discover trust and wholeness again.

Prayer:

Heavenly Father, thank You for caring about my pain. I give You every memory of betrayal and rejection. I, _____, invite Your healing presence to mend my heart's broken places. Breathe fresh hope into my relationships, and teach me to trust again. In Jesus' name, amen.

Action Step:
- Write down the names of those who hurt you. One by one, pray for them, asking God to heal your heart and bless theirs.

Daily Declarations & Affirmations:
- I declare that God is mending every wound from past hurts.
- I affirm forgiveness and release bitterness into God's hands.
- I speak life over my future relationships, trusting God's redemptive power.

Day 17: Overcoming Divorce & Separation

Malachi 2:16 (KJV)

"For the LORD, the God of Israel, saith that he hateth putting away."

Reflection:

God's heart grieves the brokenness that comes with divorce and separation. Yet even in these painful times, He offers mercy and restoration. I can find comfort knowing He is near the contrite and provides new beginnings where hope seemed lost.

Prayer:

Lord, You see the hurt and struggles caused by divorce or separation. I pray for healing and reconciliation wherever possible. I, _____, surrender the confusion, pain, and regrets. Please guide me into Your peace and lead me toward wholeness. In Jesus' name, amen.

Action Step:
- Seek biblical counseling or pastoral guidance to navigate emotional and practical challenges related to separation or divorce.

Daily Declarations & Affirmations:
- I declare God's grace covers my past, present, and future.
- I affirm hope arises in me for new seasons of life.
- I proclaim I am not defined by divorce but by God's unconditional love.

Day 18: Prayers for Fatherhood & Raising Godly Children

Proverbs 22:6 (KJV)

"Train up a child in the way he should go: and when he is old, he will not depart from it."

Reflection:

As a father, I hold a sacred trust to guide my children toward God's purposes. Consistency in love, discipline, and biblical truth can lay a firm foundation. My faithful example speaks volumes about God's character and love.

Prayer:

Heavenly Father, thank You for entrusting me with the gift of fatherhood. Teach me to model integrity, compassion, and faith before my children. I, _____, depend on Your wisdom to nurture them into godly men and women. Help me represent Your fatherly heart every day. In Jesus' name, amen.

Action Step:

- Have a special "dad date" with each child—listening, speaking life, and sharing Scripture that inspires them.

Daily Declarations & Affirmations:

- I declare my children are blessed and highly favored of the Lord.
- I affirm that God gives me the wisdom to guide them rightly.
- I proclaim our household will serve the Lord faithfully.

Day 19: Prayers for Finding a Godly Wife (For Single Men)

Proverbs 18:22 (KJV)

"Whoso findeth a wife findeth a good thing, and obtaineth favour of the LORD."

Reflection:

Marriage is a divine gift, and God delights in guiding me toward a partner who loves Him wholeheartedly. As I pray and position my heart in purity and wisdom, I trust God to bring the right woman into my life in His perfect timing.

Prayer:

Father, I trust You to orchestrate my future marriage according to Your will. Align my steps with the woman You've designed for me. I, _____, choose to honor You with my conduct, preparing myself to be a godly husband. I lay down impatience and trust Your perfect plan. In Jesus' name, amen.

Action Step:

- Focus on personal growth—spiritually, emotionally, and financially. Seek mentorship from a married believer who can guide you in becoming a strong husband-to-be.

Daily Declarations & Affirmations:

- I declare that God is directing my path toward the right spouse.
- I affirm I am becoming the kind of man a godly woman desires.
- I speak favor over my relationships and friendships, trusting God's plan.

Day 20: Breaking Free from Sexual Temptations
(Lust, Pornography, Masturbation, Adultery, Fornication, etc.)

1 Corinthians 6:18 (KJV)

"Flee fornication. Every sin that a man doeth is without the body; but he that committeth fornication sinneth against his own body."

Reflection:

Sexual sin can enslave, but God offers real freedom. Running from temptation means drawing boundaries that safeguard my heart and mind. God's standard of purity is life-giving and powerful when I rely on the Holy Spirit to transform my desires.

Prayer:

Lord, I acknowledge my struggles with sexual temptation. I repent of every sinful practice and thought. I, _____, ask for Your cleansing power to purify my heart. Help me set healthy boundaries and walk in true freedom. In Jesus' name, amen.

Action Step:

- Identify triggers and remove them—uninstall problematic apps, change daily habits, or find an accountability partner. Establish clear, God-honoring boundaries.

Daily Declarations & Affirmations:
- I declare I am set free by Christ's power from every sexual stronghold.
- I affirm that my body is a temple of the Holy Spirit.
- I proclaim purity in thoughts, actions, and desires, by God's grace.

Day 21: Healing from the Pain of an Absent Father or Broken Home

Psalm 27:10 (KJV)

"When my father and my mother forsake me, then the LORD will take me up."

Reflection:

An absent father or a broken home can create deep emotional scars, but God promises to take me in. His perfect love fills every gap in my life story. He redeems my past and reshapes my identity as His beloved son.

Prayer:

Heavenly Father, thank You for adopting me into Your family. I surrender the wounds from my childhood and the pain of an absent father. I, _____, choose to receive Your healing and acceptance. Fill my heart with the truth that You are my unfailing Father. In Jesus' name, amen.

Action Step:

- Speak to a mentor or godly friend about your experiences. Talking through past hurts can release healing and provide a new perspective.

Daily Declarations & Affirmations:
- I declare the Lord is my everlasting Father, who never leaves me.
- I affirm my worth and identity are secured in Christ.
- I speak restoration over my story, confident God is turning ashes into beauty.

PART 4: SPIRITUAL WARFARE, DELIVERANCE & FINANCIAL BREAKTHROUGH

Day 22: Breaking Generational Curses & Family Strongholds

Galatians 3:13 (KJV)

"Christ hath redeemed us from the curse of the law, being made a curse for us."

Reflection:

Jesus' sacrifice on the cross broke every curse hovering over my family line. He took upon Himself the weight of sin and every generational bondage. Through Christ's redemption, I stand free from inherited struggles, negativity, and patterns of defeat. My family story is redefined by His blood and the power of His Spirit.

Prayer:

Heavenly Father, thank You for sending Jesus to break every curse in my family. I acknowledge Your authority over my bloodline and receive the freedom You offer. I, _____, renounce every stronghold passed down to me, and I declare that my family walks in the blessings of God henceforth. In Jesus' name, amen.

Action Step:

- Write out any recurring negative patterns you see in your family. Pray over each one, specifically renouncing it in Jesus' name. Then destroy that list as a sign of release.

Daily Declarations & Affirmations

- I declare that Christ's blood has redeemed my family line.
- I affirm that every curse is broken and replaced with God's abundant blessings.
- I proclaim a new spiritual legacy of righteousness, favor, and joy.

Day 23: Deliverance from Financial Bondage & Debt

Deuteronomy 28:12 (KJV)

"The LORD shall open unto thee his good treasure, the heaven to give the rain unto thy land in his season, and to bless all the work of thine hand."

Reflection:

God's covenant promise includes provision and blessing. Though I may face seasons of lack, I stand on His Word that He opens the heavens in my behalf. By honoring His principles of stewardship and obedience, I can break free from bondage to debt and see the Lord supply every need.

Prayer:

Gracious Lord, thank You for being my ultimate provider. I reject the weight of debt and every form of financial oppression. I, _____, commit to align my finances with Your Word. Let Your favor rest on all my work, and grant me the wisdom to manage resources for Your glory. In Jesus' name, amen.

Action Step:

- Set a simple budget this week and commit to tracking every expense. Ask God for direction on reducing debt and increasing generosity.

Daily Declarations & Affirmations:

- I declare that God supplies all my needs according to His riches in glory.
- I affirm that I am a faithful steward of the resources entrusted to me.
- I speak a release from every financial stronghold and embrace divine abundance.

Day 24: Overcoming Witchcraft & Spiritual Oppression

Isaiah 54:17 (KJV)

"No weapon that is formed against thee shall prosper; and every tongue that shall rise against thee in judgment thou shalt condemn."

Reflection:

The enemy may attempt to use witchcraft, curses, or spiritual manipulation, but God's Word is clear: Such weapons cannot succeed against me. Covered by the protection of Jesus' name and fortified by the Holy Spirit, I walk in authority and victory over every dark scheme.

Prayer:

Mighty God, I praise You for being my protector. By the power of the cross, I cancel every form of witchcraft, spell, and negative word spoken against me. I, _____, break free from every chain of spiritual oppression. Let Your light dispel all darkness around me. In Jesus' mighty name, amen.

Action Step:
- Pray over your home, anointing doorposts and windows with oil if you can, declaring your space as holy ground dedicated to the Lord's presence.

Daily Declarations & Affirmations:
- I declare I am covered by the blood of Jesus and no evil power can touch me.
- I affirm that every demonic plan against me is dismantled.
- I stand in the victory Christ won, and I walk in bold spiritual authority.

Day 25: Prayers for Strength Against the Enemy's Attacks

Ephesians 6:10–12 (KJV)

"Finally, my brethren, be strong in the Lord, and in the power of his might. Put on the whole armour of God... For we wrestle not against flesh and blood, but against principalities, against powers... against spiritual wickedness in high places."

Reflection:

My real battles are not against people or circumstances but against spiritual forces that seek to derail my destiny. God has equipped me with armor—His truth, righteousness, faith, salvation, the gospel of peace, and the sword of the Spirit. Relying on His strength, I am empowered to withstand every assault.

Prayer:

Lord, I recognize the true nature of my battles. Clothe me in Your armor and strengthen me from within. I, _____, choose to stand firm, using the spiritual weapons You've provided. By Your mighty power, I resist every attack and remain steadfast in faith. In Jesus' name, amen.

Action Step:
- Each morning, intentionally pray through each piece of the Armor of God (Ephesians 6). Speak it out loud, acknowledging God's protection over every area of your life.

Daily Declarations & Affirmations
- I declare that I am strong in the Lord and in His mighty power.

- I affirm that the weapons of my warfare are divinely powerful.
- I proclaim that no attack can prevail because I stand secure in God's truth.

Day 26: Breaking Free from Addiction

(Drugs, Alcohol, Gambling, Porn, etc.)

John 8:36 (KJV)

"If the Son therefore shall make you free, ye shall be free indeed."

Reflection:

Addictions bind the mind, body, and spirit. Yet Christ's gift of freedom is stronger than any chain of dependency. By surrendering every habit to Him and seeking accountability, I can experience true deliverance and walk in the liberty that only Jesus provides.

Prayer:

Lord Jesus, You are my Deliverer. I bring every addiction and hidden struggle into Your light. I, _____, believe that Your power sets me free, and I reject the lie that I must remain in bondage. Cleanse my desires and renew my mind so I walk in lasting freedom. In Jesus' name, amen.

Action Step:
- Seek out an accountability partner or a support group. Confess your struggle and commit to walking together in prayer and practical steps toward freedom.

Daily Declarations & Affirmations:
- I declare that addiction has no hold on me because Christ sets me free.
- I affirm that my body is a temple of the Holy Spirit, and I choose purity daily.
- I speak self-control and discipline over every area of my life.

Day 27: Restoration of Lost Glory & Divine Favor

Joel 2:25 (KJV)

"And I will restore to you the years that the locust hath eaten."

Reflection:

Sometimes I feel as though I've lost seasons of my life to setbacks, failures, or spiritual attacks. But God promises to restore what was devoured. His favor isn't a fleeting moment; it's a grace that can bring a bountiful harvest even out of barren ground. I trust in His power to revive every withered place in my life.

Prayer:

Father, I thank You for being the God of restoration. I trust You to restore every lost moment, opportunity, and blessing. I, _____, receive Your divine favor and believe that You are turning my story around. Let my life testify to Your power to renew and rebuild. In Jesus' name, amen.

Action Step:
- Identify one area of your life where you've experienced loss or setback. Ask God for clarity and direction on how to move forward, believing wholeheartedly in His power to restore.

Daily Declarations & Affirmations:
- I declare God's favor opens doors that no man can shut.
- I affirm that the Lord is my restorer, and He revives every dry place in my life.
- I proclaim that in Christ, my latter days will overflow with greater blessings.

Day 28: Breaking the Spirit of Rejection & Abandonment

Romans 8:15 (KJV)

"For ye have not received the spirit of bondage again to fear; but ye have received the Spirit of adoption, whereby we cry, Abba, Father."

Reflection:

Rejection can pierce the deepest parts of my heart, leading to fear and isolation. Yet God adopts me as His own, calling me a beloved son. I am never truly abandoned; my identity is secure in His family. His perfect love eradicates every sense of rejection I've carried.

Prayer:

Abba Father, thank You for adopting me as Your child. I renounce every spirit of rejection and abandon the lies that say I am unwanted. I, _____, embrace the truth of Your love that affirms I am accepted and adored in Your sight. Teach me to rest in the warmth of Your embrace. In Jesus' name, amen.

Action Step:
- Speak aloud three truths about your acceptance in Christ. For instance, "I am chosen, I am loved, I am valuable." Let them combat any lingering feelings of rejection.

Daily Declarations & Affirmations:
- I declare I am no longer an orphan; I belong to God's family.
- I affirm that rejection has no power over me because I am fully accepted by my heavenly Father.
- I proclaim my worth is found in God's love, not in people's approval.

Day 29: Healing from Church Hurt & Religious Manipulation

Hebrews 12:15 (KJV)

"Looking diligently lest any man fail of the grace of God; lest any root of bitterness springing up trouble you, and thereby many be defiled."

Reflection

Past hurts within church communities can create deep wounds and bitterness. Yet God calls you to pursue peace and extend grace—first receiving it from Him, then offering it to others. Church hurt is not a reflection of God's character; it's a reminder that people, even in faith circles, can fall short. Christ offers complete healing so you can move forward unburdened.

Prayer

Heavenly Father, today I surrender the hurts I've experienced in church settings. I lay every disappointment at Your feet. I, _____, trust You to heal my wounds and remove any bitterness that lingers in my heart. Teach me to forgive and walk in love as You have forgiven me. Help me see Your family— the Church—through Your eyes of compassion. In Jesus' name, amen.

Action Step

- Pray specifically for individuals or leaders who have hurt you. Ask God to bless them and help you release any grudges. If possible, prayerfully consider reconciling or extending a gesture of peace.

Daily Declarations & Affirmations

- I declare that bitterness has no hold on my heart.
- I affirm that God's grace is sufficient to heal every wound.
- I choose forgiveness, releasing every offense to Christ.

Day 30: Prayers for Spiritual Strength & Growth in Faith

Jude 1:20 (KJV)

"But ye, beloved, building up yourselves on your most holy faith, praying in the Holy Ghost."

Reflection

Faith is like a muscle—it grows as it's challenged and exercised. Praying in the Spirit and abiding in God's Word fortifies your resolve, renews your mind, and aligns your heart with God's will. In this final day, remember that spiritual empowerment is an ongoing journey. Continue stepping forward in the strength of the Holy Spirit, confident in God's faithful guidance.

Prayer

Mighty God, thank You for every step that has brought me here. I, _____, desire to keep growing stronger in faith, grounded in Your truth. Fill me anew with Your Holy Spirit. Grant me wisdom, courage, and the perseverance to stand firm amid every challenge. I commit to a lifetime of seeking Your heart and shining Your light. In Jesus' powerful name, amen.

Action Step

• Identify one spiritual discipline (such as daily Bible reading, consistent prayer times, or fellowship with other believers) and set a clear plan to grow deeper in it this coming month.

Daily Declarations & Affirmations

- I declare that my faith is continually strengthened by God's Word.
- I affirm that I walk in the power of the Holy Spirit daily.
- I proclaim that I am a man of unwavering faith and courage in Christ.

Five Spiritual Exercises for Men

Each exercise is rooted in Scripture and addresses various aspects of a man's spiritual journey, from identity and emotional healing to relationships, deliverance, and spiritual empowerment.

1. Fasting for Breakthrough and Deliverance

Scriptural Foundation:

- **Matthew 17:21** – "However, this kind does not go out except by prayer and fasting."
- **Isaiah 58:6** – "Is not this the fast that I have chosen: to loose the bands of wickedness, to undo the heavy burdens, and to let the oppressed go free, and that ye break every yoke?"

Purpose:
Fasting is a spiritual discipline that strengthens a man's spirit, helps break strongholds, and brings clarity to his purpose. Many struggles in identity, stagnation, addiction, and generational curses can be fought effectively through fasting.

How to Practice:

- Choose a specific fast (water fast, Daniel fast, intermittent fasting).
- Set a clear purpose for the fast (breaking generational curses, career breakthrough, deliverance from sexual strongholds, etc.).

- Spend dedicated time in prayer and reading Scripture while fasting.
- Avoid distractions such as excessive entertainment or social media.
- Keep a prayer journal to document insights and victories received during the fast.

Spiritual Benefit:

Fasting brings supernatural breakthrough, deeper intimacy with God, and divine intervention in areas of spiritual warfare.

2. Prayer Walks for Spiritual Warfare & Victory

Scriptural Foundation:

- **Joshua 1:3** – "Every place that the sole of your foot shall tread upon, that have I given unto you, as I said unto Moses."
- **Ephesians 6:12** – "For we wrestle not against flesh and blood, but against principalities, against powers, against the rulers of the darkness of this world, against spiritual wickedness in high places."

Purpose:
Prayer walks allow men to declare God's promises over their lives, homes, workplaces, and communities. Walking and praying in faith strengthens spiritual authority and disrupts demonic strongholds.

How to Practice:

- Choose specific locations to pray over (home, neighborhood, workplace).
- Declare God's promises out loud while walking.
- Bind and cast out any demonic presence that may be influencing those areas.
- Use Scripture-based declarations of victory over every area of life.
- Engage in group prayer walks for added spiritual strength and accountability.

Spiritual Benefit:

Prayer walks establish spiritual authority, help men take dominion in their environments, and reinforce the habit of bold, faith-filled prayer.

3. Accountability Partnerships for Purity and Growth

Scriptural Foundation:

- **Proverbs 27:17** – "Iron sharpeneth iron; so a man sharpeneth the countenance of his friend."
- **James 5:16** – "Confess your faults one to another, and pray one for another, that ye may be healed."

Purpose:
Accountability is a powerful weapon against secret sin, stagnation, and deception. It ensures men stay grounded, supported, and encouraged in their spiritual walk.

How to Practice:

- Choose a spiritually mature accountability partner.
- Set up a weekly or biweekly check-in to discuss struggles and victories.
- Be honest and open about areas of temptation, spiritual dryness, or personal battles.
- Engage in mutual prayer, fasting, and encouragement.
- Establish clear action steps to overcome struggles (e.g., removing digital temptations, limiting access to harmful environments, memorizing Scripture together).

Spiritual Benefit:

Accountability helps men break free from isolation, build godly habits, and sustain their spiritual momentum.

4. Daily Declarations & Affirmations for Identity & Confidence

Scriptural Foundation:

- **Proverbs 18:21** – "Death and life are in the power of the tongue: and they that love it shall eat the fruit thereof."
- **2 Corinthians 5:17** – "Therefore, if any man be in Christ, he is a new creature: old things are passed away; behold, all things are become new."

Purpose:
Speaking God's Word daily strengthens a man's identity,

confidence, and authority. Declarations break the lies of the enemy and reinforce God's truth in a man's heart.

How to Practice:

- Start each morning with five minutes of biblical declarations.
- Speak Scripture-based affirmations over identity, family, career, finances, and purity.
- Reject every lie of the enemy and replace it with a biblical truth.
- Create personalized declarations that address specific struggles.
- Stand in front of a mirror or write declarations down to visualize them.

Example Declarations:

- "I am a new creation in Christ; my past does not define me!"
- "I am more than a conqueror through Christ!"
- "I walk in purity, self-control, and spiritual authority."
- "No weapon formed against me shall prosper!"

Spiritual Benefit:

Daily declarations reshape thought patterns, build confidence, and reinforce spiritual strength against the enemy's lies.

5. Midnight Prayers for Spiritual Breakthrough

Scriptural Foundation:

- **Psalm 119:62** – "At midnight I will rise to give thanks unto thee because of thy righteous judgments."
- **Acts 16:25-26** – "And at midnight Paul and Silas prayed, and sang praises unto God: and the prisoners heard them. And suddenly there was a great earthquake, so that the foundations of the prison were shaken."

Purpose:
Midnight prayers are a powerful way to engage in spiritual warfare and break demonic cycles of delay, oppression, and bondage.

How to Practice:

- Dedicate at least one or two nights a week to midnight prayer (12 AM–3 AM).
- Focus on prayers of deliverance, generational breaking, and divine restoration.
- Sing praises before and after prayer as a weapon of spiritual warfare.
- Use targeted warfare prayers against stagnation, financial lack, addiction, or family bondage.
- Engage in intercessory prayer for your household, children, and future generations.

Spiritual Benefit:

Midnight prayers break spiritual barriers, accelerate breakthroughs, and release divine intervention in areas of oppression.

Conclusion: Walking in Continuous Victory

Spiritual warfare is not a one-time battle but a lifelong journey. The enemy constantly seeks to undermine men in their faith, relationships, and purpose, but God has provided powerful weapons to ensure victory. By engaging in **fasting, prayer walks, accountability partnerships, declarations, and midnight prayers**, men can live as **warriors, not victims**.

Jesus has already won the battle (Colossians 2:15), but it is up to each man to **stand firm, resist the enemy (James 4:7), and claim the promises of God**. Victory is not just a hope—it is a reality in Christ.

"Put on the whole armor of God, that ye may be able to stand against the wiles of the devil." — **Ephesians 6:11**

Men of God, rise and walk in the power, purity, and authority that Christ has given you!

www.ingramcontent.com/pod-product-compliance
Lightning Source LLC
Chambersburg PA
CBHW061718120626
46550CB00003B/1277